Our Neighbour's a Vampire!

Adam Guillain

Illustrated by Francis Blake

Ginn

William was standing on the sofa. He looked wild. His hair was a mess and there was a shifty look in his eyes. He was playing 'spies'. It was the game where he pretended to be a secret agent, like James Bond. William used his dad's binoculars to look through the front window. In the street, three men were unloading a van.

"You're being nosy again," said Dad.

"But I'm on lookout," said William.

It was getting dark outside. William watched as an old, black car pulled up next door.

"This must be our new neighbour," said William.

William looked through the binoculars again. He watched a strange man in a long, black raincoat get out of the car. William felt the hairs on the back of his neck stand on end.

The man had a long, crooked nose and pointy ears. His head was as smooth as a pebble, but he had the longest black beard William had ever seen.

William nearly jumped out of his skin when the man turned his big, bulging eyeballs towards him.

"Scary," thought William. He ducked under the windowsill and made notes in his little black book.

DAY ONE
NEW NEIGHBOUR!
BLACK RAINCOAT
OLD TRAINERS
LOOKS SHIFTY!
CRIMINAL?
WIZARD??!

William peered over the windowsill just as the man lifted a long, black box from the boot of his car. William shivered. "A coffin!" he thought.

William's dad was getting cross. "Come for dinner," he said firmly.

William left his lookout and stomped off to the kitchen.

As soon as he had eaten his dinner, William took the binoculars upstairs. He jumped on to his bed and peered through the curtains.

"This is better," he thought.

Next door, his new neighbour was dragging the long, black box into the garden shed.

"What's he up to?" thought William.

Just then, he thought he saw witches in the red sky. He looked up through the binoculars, but it was just a flock of geese. He watched them fly off over the woods.

William wanted to stay and watch, but it was time for his bath. He was just getting out of the bath when he heard wild flapping outside. "What was that?" he wondered.

Later, just before bedtime, he heard another noise outside. He pulled back his bedroom curtains.

Next door, his new neighbour was climbing over the back fence.

"Why is he heading for the woods?" William said to himself.

Just before he turned out the light, William wrote in his book.

> DAY ONE
> LATE AT NIGHT!
> COFFIN!
> LOUD FLAPS AFTER DARK!
> NEIGHBOUR GOES TO WOODS!!

These were the thoughts in William's head as he fell asleep.

Soon after William had fallen asleep, he woke up in a hot sweat. "He's a vampire!" he thought.

He switched on the light and pulled back his curtains. The moon made long shadows over the lawn.

Suddenly, William realised that the light from his window had given him away. His neighbour was standing in the middle of his garden looking right up at him!

William ran to the top of the stairs and shouted, "Help! Our neighbour's a vampire!"

William's parents were still downstairs. "Get back to bed," his mum called.

"You never believe me," William grumbled.

By the time he got back to the window, there was nothing to see.

11

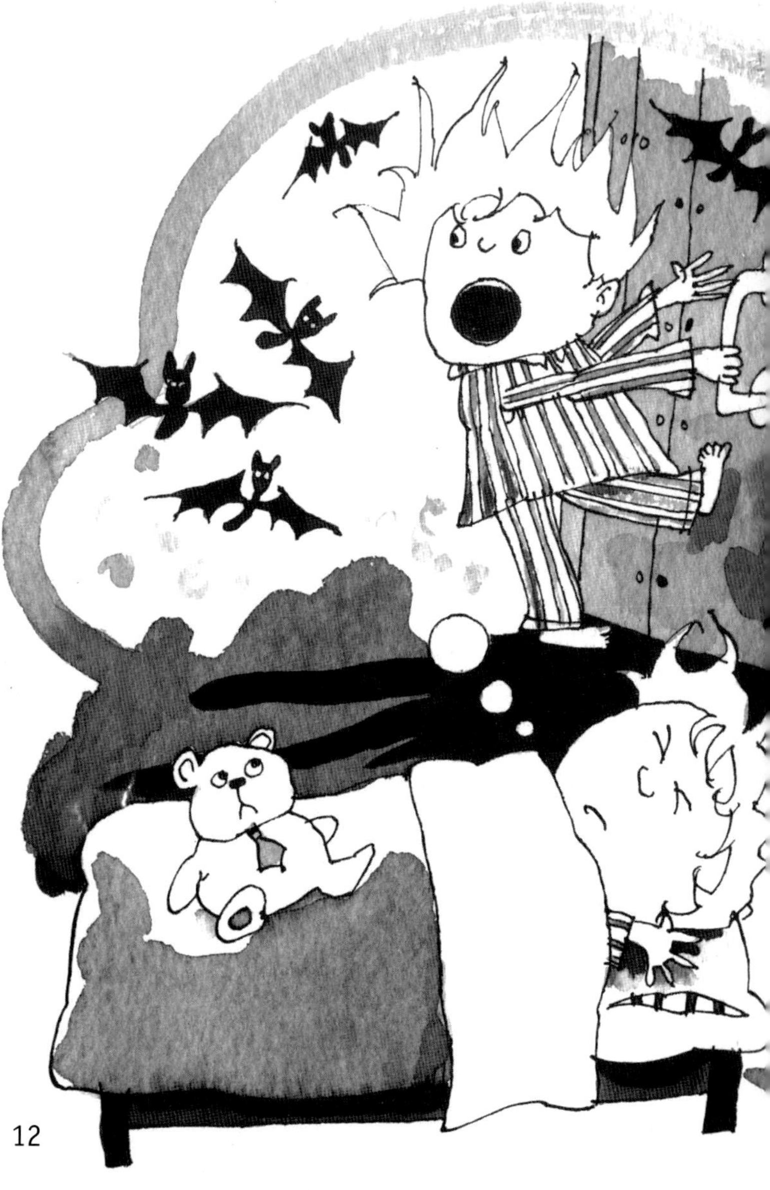

William fell asleep again, but he slept badly. He had a bad dream about a vampire. In his dream, the vampire had trapped him in a room full of bats.

"William, are you all right?" asked Mum. She was standing beside his bed. "It sounds like you were having a nightmare."

William was happy to find himself back in his own bed, and not in the room full of bats.

"Our neighbour's a vampire," William told his mum. "And I'm going to prove it."

The next day was hard for William. He knew his neighbour had seen him spying at the window. William was sure the vampire was going to come and get him.

He went to school and wrote a report to give to the police.

"I thought we were all writing a story about pirates today," said his teacher.

"I wrote a story about pirates last year," William told her.

William's teacher sighed and let him finish his report.

After school, William gave the report to his mum. "Please will you give that to the police if anything happens to me?" he asked.

"What would happen to you?" asked his mum.

"I might be attacked by bats, or killed by a vampire," said William.

"You and your imagination!" sighed Mum.

That night, William made a plan.

He knew that good spies took photos and they used them to prove things.

Tomorrow would be Saturday. His mum and dad let him stay up until nine o'clock.

William knew that there was a gap in the hedge at the bottom of his garden. He used the gap when he wanted to get his football back from next door. Mrs Patel, who had lived there before, had said it was okay.

On Saturday night, William was ready.

"Mum, can I take my telescope to the bottom of the garden tonight?" William asked.

"Okay. But don't forget to put your coat on," Mum said.

Before William set off, he got a torch and his mum's camera. He knew vampires hated garlic so he put some in his coat pocket.

"Just to be on the safe side," William thought.

It was already dark when William pulled himself through the hedge into his neighbour's garden. A cold wind rustled through the trees. There was no light in the garden, but William knew where the garden shed was.

He could see the outline of the shed across the lawn and started to creep towards it. He thought about how angry his mum and dad would be if they could see him.

Suddenly, the wind blew very hard and the shed door flew open.

Shadows shot out across the garden.

William almost screamed. He dropped everything and dived behind a bush.

The sound of wild flapping burst into the night.

"Bats!" he gasped. William knew that vampires could turn into bats. He watched them fly off into the night sky.

William lay still on the ground, too scared to move. He thought about going straight home, but he really wanted to get a photo of the vampire's coffin.

William picked up
the camera and torch
and crept up to the
shed. He stepped in
through the open door
and started to look around.

William had just spotted
the long, black box in the corner
when the shed door slammed shut.

William dropped the camera and torch.
Now he was scared. It was too dark to find
the latch on the shed door. William started
to kick the door.

"Help! Vampire!" he shouted.

William tried to think what James Bond would do and started to look for the torch. With the torch, he would be able to find the latch and open the door.

"Mum! Dad!" he cried, as he looked. He kept calling and calling until his throat was sore. But no one came.

After a while, William became tired of calling and he still hadn't found the torch. He was glad he had his coat on. He did the zip up and sat down on the shed floor. If his mum and dad did not find him soon, he would be in big trouble.

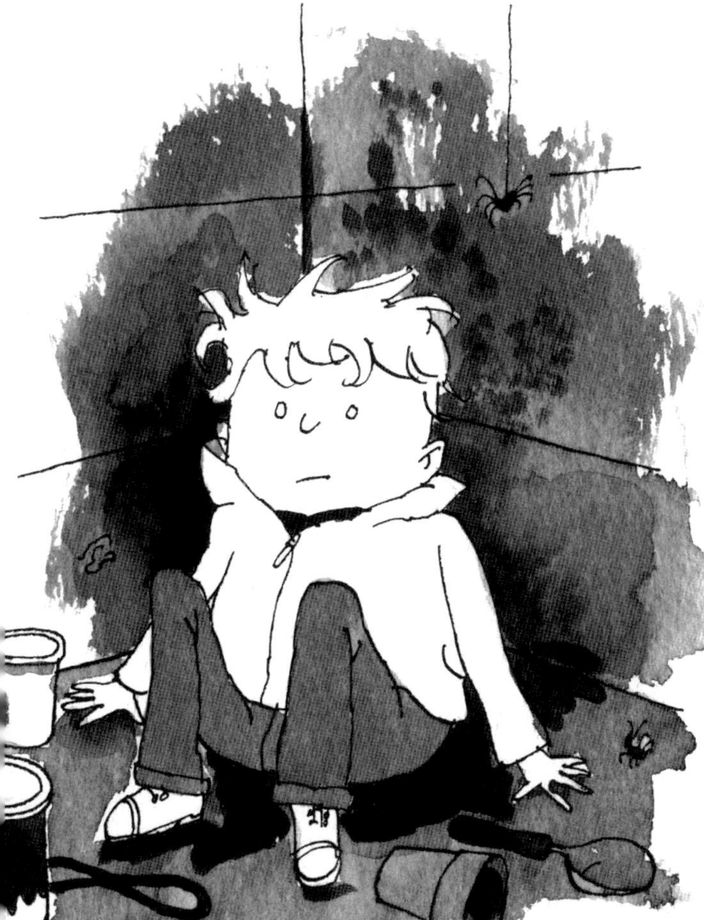

William hadn't been sitting for long when he heard a car door slam. Then he heard heavy footsteps on the lawn.

"The vampire!" he thought.

Now William was *really* scared. He jumped to his feet and pulled the garlic from his pocket. As he backed away from the door, he put his foot on something round.

"The torch!" he gasped.

He picked it up and switched it on. William hunched his shoulders. "If the vampire bites my neck, I've had it," he thought.

There was a rattling at the shed door. He was too scared even to breathe.

The door flew open.

"Aaaargh!" screamed William.

He shone the torch into the vampire's eyes and threw the garlic at him.

"Aaaargh!" screamed the dazzled vampire.

William pushed past him and ran.

He crawled through the gap in the hedge and ran across his own garden.

His mum and dad were standing by the back door. They had heard the screams.

"Help! Vampire!" William called.

"William's playing his spy game again," said Mum.

"He's been in our neighbour's garden," said Dad. He had seen William crawl back under the hedge. "I'll go and say sorry to our new neighbour," he said.

William ran past his mum and dad and up the stairs. He got his water pistol and hid under his covers. If the vampire followed him, he was ready.

But only his mum came into his bedroom.

"William, would you like some milk?" she asked.

"No! I'm on a mission," he said.

He knew that without a photo no one would believe him. Still holding the water pistol, William fell asleep.

When William woke up, his room was full of light.

"Phew! I'm safe," he sighed. William knew that vampires only came out at night.

William yawned and stretched his arms. He didn't feel like being a spy today. He got washed and changed, then went downstairs.

"William, come here," Dad called from the sitting room. William went to see what he wanted.

"William, I'd like you to meet Victor, our new neighbour," said Dad.

William's jaw fell wide open. The vampire from next door was sitting on the sofa with a cup of tea! On the table, William saw the camera he had left in his garden shed.

"He knows it was me," William trembled.

"Victor studies bats," said Dad. "He keeps some in his garden shed. If you want, we can go with him tomorrow night. He's putting up a new hide so he can watch bats in the woods."

"You can use the binoculars in the hide like a real spy," said Mum.

William was feeling dizzy.

"Who knows what else you might see!" said Victor with a smile.

William was sure he saw fangs.